Seeds & Harvest

2017

By Dr. Delron Shirley

Cover design by Jeremy Shirley

Table of Contents

PRODUCTIVE SEED	1
WHATSOEVER YOU SOW	6
FALTERING HARVEST	12
MISSIONARY SEED	18
PROPHETIC HARVEST	25
TEACH ALL NATIONS MISSION	29
BOOKS BY DELRON & PEGGY SHIRLEY	31

This teaching manual is intended for personal study; however, the author encourages all students to also become teachers and to share the truths from this text with others. However, copying the text itself without permission from the author is considered plagiarism which is punishable by law. To obtain permission to quote material from this book, please contact:

Delron Shirley
3210 Cathedral Spires Dr.
Colorado Springs, CO 80904
www.teachallnationsmission.com
teachallnations@msn.com

This little manuscript is about sowing and reaping – but before you jump to any conclusions and think, "Well, I've heard this message a million times from everybody from Oral Roberts down," let me warn you that what I'm going to share is very likely something that you've never heard before. We often talk about sowing and reaping, seeds and harvests, and seedtime and harvest time with such a mechanical approach that it is easy to get a mental image that everything happens automatically – you toss a Ben Franklin in the offering and, almost magically, the Brinks armored car pulls up to your front door with a delivery the next morning. My objective is simply to get us to start re-thinking some of our cookie-cutter ideas. So, let's take a look at the topic from some different angles.

Productive Seed

I will always remember the day. There were just four of us in the private office that day – Dr. Lester Sumrall, a husband and wife missionary team, and myself. After a brief conversation, Dr. Sumrall slid a check across his desk to my missionary friends who run feeding centers in one of the impoverished nations of Asia. Along with the check came these gruff words, "God hasn't called me to feed the devil's children, and I don't believe in this sort of thing. When I go to the mission field, I don't see naked babies. But I'm giving you this for your work because I don't want the world to say that we don't try to help people." Yes, Dr. Lester Sumrall was a man of faith who traveled around the globe setting people free from the devil's power. Yes, he had built nation-changing churches in several countries, raised up a world-wide broadcasting network, and authored scores of life-changing books. Yes, he had been in the ministry for more than fifty years and had ministered in more than a hundred nations. But, there was still one thing lacking in his ministry – compassion for humans' physical needs. However, all that was to change late one evening in Jerusalem. Shortly after retiring after a long day of touring and taping television programs followed by preaching and ministering to the tour members, he was suddenly awakened by the words, "It is not only ten minutes to midnight in Jerusalem; it is ten minutes to midnight prophetically!" For the next five hours, the Lord continued to talk with His servant concerning a new commission of establishing a global ministry to feed the hungry saints who lack their daily bread. At first, Dr. Sumrall retorted that he was seventy-five years old and that God should get a younger man to take on this job. Eventually, he understood that God had saved this job for him until this stage in life because he was now seasoned enough to take on a project of this immensity. From that moment until the day he drew his last breath, Lester Sumrall poured every ounce of energy he had into seeing that this vision would be fulfilled. Upon his return to the US a few days later, I again sat in the apostle's office and witnessed him slide a piece of paper across his desk. This time, it was a page from a yellow legal pad totally filled with the words the Lord had spoken to him that night in Jerusalem. The paper contained not just words, but also huge smears where warm tears had dissolved the ink – evidence of a heart in which a new level of pity and compassion had been birthed.

When this new element became operative in his ministry, Lester Sumrall stepped to a new level in his career as a man who made a difference in his world. Because of this new birth of pity, he was able to impact thousands on every continent of the world in the last few years of his life and bring influential change to whole nations and people groups. The words of the apostle Jude so adequately sum up the story of this chapter in Lester Sumrall's life and ministry, "Some have compassion, making a difference."

(verse 22) As Dr. Sumrall began to share his vision with the pastors and Christian leaders in America, Europe, and Australia, something phenomenal began to happen. Individuals and churches that were struggling financially began to prosper and ones that considered themselves to already be financially secure began to abound. It was as if Dr. Sumrall's vision had unlocked a new door of prosperity within the Body of Christ. And actually – it had. For the most part, the "Word and Faith Movement" churches in which Dr. Sumrall basically ministered previously had no humanitarian programs. But now that he had introduced the new Feed the Hungry program, their attention was redirected in a way that could best be described in the prayer of Bob Pierce, founder of World Vision, "Break my heart with things that break Yours." Certainly all these churches and believers were all well-versed in the principle of sowing and reaping – but something new happened in their harvests the minute they stepped across this new threshold in their planting.

    Before we go any further with that idea, let me introduce you to a hero of our generation whose name most people will never know, yet he prevented the death of at least a billion humans around the world. Norman Borlaug has been called the "Forgotten Benefactor of Humanity" because he is a fairly unknown figure even though he almost single-handedly initiated the Green Revolution by developing a form of agriculture that dramatically increased food production around the world. When he introduced the high-yielding seed varieties that he had developed – along with modern agricultural production techniques – the results were astronomical. Mexico became a net exporter of wheat, and wheat yields nearly doubled in Pakistan and India – greatly improving the food security in those nations. The thing that we have to realize about Dr. Borlaug is that he never suffered from hunger or malnutrition. Even though he had sufficient food for himself, he had a concern for those who didn't. That concern compelled him to invest all that he could into developing more productive seeds and promoting farming techniques that would produce a harvest for others – a harvest that he didn't need for himself but saved the lives of millions!

Let's contrast Dr. Borlaug with a character that we know of from the Bible:

> And he spake a parable unto them, saying, The ground of a certain rich man brought forth plentifully: And he thought within himself, saying, What shall I do, because I have no room where to bestow my fruits? And he said, This will I do: I will pull down my barns, and build greater; and there will I bestow all my fruits and my goods. And I will say to my soul, Soul, thou hast much goods laid up for many years; take thine ease, eat, drink, and be merry. But God said unto him, Thou fool, this night thy soul shall be required of thee: then whose shall those things be, which thou hast provided? So is he that layeth up treasure for himself, and is not rich toward God. (Luke 12:16-21)

This farmer produced a harvest that overflowed his barns. Notice that Jesus said that he had barns – not just one barn. Although we are not told how many barns there were or how big those barns were, we are left with the impression that he had a really huge harvest because his ground had produced plentifully and yielded enough to sustain him for many years. The point of the story is that he saw the harvest as his supply rather than a source for supplying other's needs. Although he is not directly paralleled with the rich man in another parable, he must have had at least somewhat of the same mentality that he was going to fare sumptuously with little or no regard for beggars like Lazarus who might gather outside his door and starve. (Luke 16:19-21)

The contrast between the biblical farmer of old and the modern agricultural scientist brings us to the essence of the new experience that Dr. Sumrall's ministry brought into the Body of Christ. Bountiful harvests come when we set our hearts on how to use the harvest for blessing others. Paul made this point clear when he characterized the harvest that the believers in Corinth would receive if they sowed into the lives of the poor saints in Jerusalem, "God is able to make all grace abound toward you; that ye, always having all sufficiency in all things, may abound to every good work." (II Corinthians 9:8) He promised that as they gave sacrificially to bless those in need, they would reap a harvest that would not just sustain them but also put them in a position to continue to bless others in any need that would arise at any time. It was foolish for the farmer in Luke to think of containing and retaining his blessing; however, when the Corinthians – like Dr. Borlaug and Dr. Sumrall – saw the harvest as a way to rescue others, the harvest abounded exponentially! Additionally, this kind of harvest knows no time limits. Notice that Paul said that the Corinthians would have this abounding grace always – not just at a scheduled harvest season. In other words, it will come in <u>due</u> season as Paul promised in Galatians 6:9. Pardon the pun, but we can expect the harvest to come when our bills are <u>due</u> – even if it isn't payday yet.

However, there is a basic principle that we must all remember about life – for every balloon, there is a needle. Therefore, I need to burst your bubble before you blow it up so big that it will make a really big bang. It's better to deal with the potential misapplication of this principle while it's still at the simple little popping stage. It is all too easy to grab hold of a truth like this and try to turn it into a system or simple method that we anticipate will bring automatic success – God will bless me if I feed the poor. Paul distinctly bursts that bubble in I Corinthians 13:3, "Though I bestow all my goods to feed the poor…and have not charity, it profiteth me nothing." Going through the motions without the proper motivation will not produce results. Sowing and reaping is more than the mechanics of giving. It is only when we act out of genuine compassion that we make a difference – in the lives of the hungry that we feed and in our own lives.

Whatsoever You Sow

Having discussed about Dr. Norman Borlaug and the Green Revolution, we must address one significantly related issue – the fact that we still live in a hungry world. Technically, the farmers of the world produce enough food right now to feed every one of the seven billion-plus members of the human family – yet almost eight hundred million people suffer malnutrition and nearly eight million people die of hunger or hunger-related diseases each year. Why? One of the major causes is the fact that we actually lose over half of our food supply before it gets to the table. In developing nations, much of the crops simply are not harvested or they are lost during the harvesting process. In developed nations, the losses in the fields are not as significant as the losses in transit, storage, and even in the consumers' refrigerators. Of course, this is not a modern issue. Jesus straightforwardly told the disciples that they should be prayerful about the possible – and, actually, probably – loss of the harvest, "The harvest truly is plenteous, but the labourers are few; Pray ye therefore the Lord of the harvest, that he will send forth labourers into his harvest." (Matthew 9:37-38) His words remind me of a story that a missionary friend of mine loves to share. Remembering the fun that he had as a boy in Michigan when his dad would take him to pick apples, he wanted to share the same experience with his own boys. So, when they were back from the mission field to visit Grandma one fall, my friend found a nearby apple orchard and asked the owner if he would allow the boys to pick a basketful. The owner's response was totally unexpected, "Have all you want. The trees are loaded and the ground is full of ones that have already fallen." For some reason, the migrant workers that he depended upon to harvest his orchard had failed to arrive that season – and his entire harvest was going to rot! My missionary friend says that this experience sent him back to the mission field with a renewed vision to bring in the souls in that nation before it was too late.

This use of harvest symbolism to speak of the souls of men brings us to another significant truth that we must understand if we want to have a biblical view on sowing and reaping – it's not all (and sometimes, not at all) about money. We all too often truncate the seed-harvest message by limiting it to money. Yes, it does apply to finances; Paul specifically used the imagery to talk about money in II Corinthians chapters eight and nine; however, when Jesus gave the parable of the sower, He point-blankly interpreted the seed to be – not money – but the Word of God (Matthew 13:19, 13:20, 13:22, 13:23; Luke 8:11), the harvest to be souls of men (John 4:35), the sower to be – not a person in the church pew – but the Son of Man Himself (Matthew 13:37), and the things that were given to be love, blessings, prayer, good deeds, mercy, and judgment as distinctly as money (Luke 6:27-38). The Apostle Peter spoke of an incorruptible seed – the word of God – that would produce the harvest of our new birth. (I Peter 1:23) It's also interesting that from cover to cover the Bible repeatedly refers to our children as our seed. (Genesis 3:15, Revelation 12:17) Furthermore, Paul used the sowing and reaping symbolism to speak of positive and negative spiritual actions and attitudes. (Galatians 6:7-9)

It must have been a sight to see – one of the city leaders walking around town with one shoe on and one shoe off. Children pointed and giggled, women snickered behind their shawls as they tried to appear not to be looking, and men used the occasion to poke ribald jokes and insults at their friend. When Boaz had caught a glimpse of the beautiful young lady working in his field, he was immediately smitten – even though he took a bit of a circuitous route before he admitted it. But once he realized the value of the damsel who slipped into the threshing floor to draw out his true emotions, he began to pursue her. His kinsman – who was actually one position closer to Naomi and, therefore, first in line to redeem Naomi's inheritance and marry Ruth – failed to see that the real harvest this season was not barley, but the beautiful gleaner among the barley spikes. Not realizing the treasure that was within his grasp, he lost his chance at the harvest. (Ruth 4:1-12) But, he not only lost his chance, he also lost his shoe in a ceremonial release of the inheritance to Boaz. Certainly, the thing that made the children giggle, the women snicker, and the men laugh out loud was his humiliating stroll through the city square with only one shoe, but the real embarrassment of the story was the fact that he actually had a treasure in his grasp and lost it because he didn't realize that it was a harvest ready to be collected.

The very idea of paralleling reaping a harvest with the possibility that Boaz's relative could have had a chance to redeem Naomi's inheritance brings up the question of how could he have reaped such a harvest without having planted any seeds for it. Technically, everything that is sown will be reaped – but often not by the sower. Let's look at a few examples. Jesus taught us that the ravens (symbolic of the devil) will gobble up the seed as soon as it is sown if it is sown on the bad soil of the pathway. (Matthew 13:19) He also taught us that some of the seed we sow fails to reach maturity because the shallow soil prohibits it from taking root or because the weeds smother it. It may seem to be a stretch of the imagination, but in these cases the sun and the weeds got the harvest. We also read about crops that actually grow to maturity but are eaten by locusts. (Joel 1:4) Somebody – even if it was a thief – got the harvest! So we see, the first principle concerning failing to reap – diligence to protect our crop from the elements and thieves. Someone is going to get the harvest, but it may not go to the legitimate owner if he is not cautious.

Actually, it is often true that a harvest is reaped by an individual who did not actually sow for that harvest. This is actually a biblical principle. In Matthew 25:26, Luke 9:22, and John 4:38, we find explicit statements concerning reaping even when we have not sown. Let's explore a couple reasons why this can happen.

Peggy Brown saved Kevin Stephan's life when she was able to use CPR after he was injured in a Little League baseball game. Years later, he saved her life by administering the Heimlich maneuver when she choked on food in a restaurant where he worked. Hearing this story leaves us all shaking our heads, wondering, "What are the odds?" Actually, the probability of such a coincidence happening is incredibly small. Yet, we may fail to apply the same mentality to the principle of sowing and reaping – but if we did, we would realize that we should not always look for our harvest in the same place we sow our seeds.

The first reason that we reap where we haven't sown is that the we have actually sown – just in other fields. Ruth was able to reap in Boaz's fields because she had sown into Naomi's life. (Ruth 1:16-17) The meek can inherit the earth (Psalm 37:11, Matthew 5:5) because they are rich toward

God (Revelation 2:9). The Israelites were able to take possession of fields they didn't plant and houses they didn't build when they came into the Promised Land (Deuteronomy 6:10-11) because they had built cities for the Egyptians (Exodus 1:11). The rich master whose servant acknowledged that he reaped where he hadn't sown had sown elsewhere – into the lives of his servants. (Matthew 25:15) In our own lives, we need to realize that our harvest will often come from an unexpected source as we reap from fields where we haven't sown even though we may not see an increase from the specific planting we have done in other fields. Jesus taught us this principle in Luke 6:38 when He said, "Give, and it shall be given unto you; good measure, pressed down, and shaken together, and running over, shall men give into your bosom." Notice that He didn't say that the same person to whom we give will the one who gives back to us. In fact, in the very context of this statement He made it clear that receiving back from the same individuals to whom we give is contrary to His kingdom's strategies. (Luke 6:32-33) With this truth in mind, it is important to heed the advice of King Solomon, "Cast thy bread upon the waters: for thou shalt find it after many days. Give a portion to seven, and also to eight; for thou knowest not what evil shall be upon the earth" (Ecclesiastes 11:1-2) – plant diversely because we never know exactly which field will produce the most abundant harvest.

  The second reason that we can reap where we haven't sown is that – because of God's abundant grace – the harvest is so plenteous that it can't possibly be reaped by just those who sowed into it. Amos 9:13 speaks of a time when plowman will overtake the reaper and the ones who tread the grapes will overrun the one who is planting in the vineyards. The imagery here is that the land will be so productive that the normal pattern of seedtime and harvest will be disrupted. Reapers will have to rush to get out of the way of the ones who are readying the field for the next planting and the sowers will be in the way of those who are gathering grapes and making wine. In the abundance of the harvest, there is total confusion as to who is reaping from whose seed.

Thus, it clear that we are to reap what we sow (Proverbs 22:8, II Corinthians 9:6, Galatians 6:7-8), but we are to also reap what others have sown. The Old Testament law demanded that produce be left in the fields at harvest time for the specific purpose of providing for those in need. (Leviticus 19:10, Deuteronomy 24:21) The best example of this principle in action is a story that we have already visited a couple times – Ruth who fed herself and her mother-in-law by gleaning in the field of Boaz. Another example was the entrance of the people of Israel into the land of Canaan where they took possessions of gardens, orchards, vineyards, and fields that they did not plant. God sometimes allows us to benefit from the labors of others as a bonus in our lives. Additionally, there is a divine harvest in which we reap a harvest from the seeds that God Himself has sown. In fact, this was the original pattern in that the human race was originally designed to reap from seeds that God Himself planted. The Bible tells us that God planted a garden in Eden and then appointed our ancestral parents – Adam and Eve – as caretakers in the garden that He had planted for them. His instructions were that they could harvest all the bounty of the garden – except, of course, the one special tree, "Out of the ground made the LORD God to grow every tree that is pleasant to the sight, and good for food...And the LORD God commanded the man, saying, Of every tree of the garden thou mayest freely eat." (Genesis 2:8-16) Matthew 13:37 tells us that the sower in the oft-quoted parable is actually the Son of Man, not the believer. The bottom line to this truth is that all the good things that come into our lives are actually the result of the seed that God sowed when He sent Jesus to earth and the subsequent seed that Jesus sowed when He went to the cross. (John 12:24)

Faltering Harvest

The two operations of sowing and reaping are often segregated from one another. There are some forms of sowing that are actually more enjoyable – at least to our carnal side – than the reaping associated with them. In such cases, people often want to sow but have no intention of ever reaping. This would be what we call "sowing wild oats." Much of our society today wants to sow without reaping the consequences. For example, having casual sex has become commonplace and is just part of the current social norm. However, those who participate have little or no concern for the consequences such as unwanted pregnancies or sexually transmitted diseases. When such consequences do result, there is a ready solution that also ignores the consequences that it brings. For example, an abortion will eliminate the problem of the unwanted pregnancy, but it begins a whole new cycle of consequences as the woman must deal with the inner guilt it produces. We may question this whole discussion with the objection that we are not involved in casual sex and certainly not advocating abortion. However, we may still need to stop and consider the other less obvious seeds that we may have planted without considering the harvest that they are destined to produce. Bad attitudes can be just as disastrous as bad actions, but we often ignore the fact that they will eventually produce emotional – and possibly even a physical – harvests. Anger, prejudice, resentment, and other negative attitudes held inside our hearts will cause emotional stress and often even physical diseases.

Jesus taught us to sow without expecting a harvest but to be aware that we would certainly receive one.

> But love ye your enemies, and do good, and lend, hoping for nothing again; and your reward shall be great, and ye shall be the children of the Highest: for he is kind unto the unthankful and to the evil. Be ye therefore merciful, as your Father also is merciful. Judge not, and ye shall not be judged: condemn not, and ye shall not be condemned: forgive, and ye shall be forgiven: Give, and it shall be given unto you; good measure, pressed down, and shaken together, and running over, shall men give into your bosom. For with the same measure that ye mete withal it shall be measured to you again. (Luke 6:35-38)

Paul taught us to generously sow good deeds. "Be not deceived; God is not mocked: for whatsoever a man soweth, that shall he also reap. For he that soweth to his flesh shall of the flesh reap corruption; but he that soweth to the Spirit shall of the Spirit reap life everlasting. And let us not be weary in well doing: for in due season we shall reap, if we faint not. As we have therefore opportunity, let us do good unto all men, especially unto them who are of the household of faith." (Galatians 6:7-10)

If you sow, you'll reap; if not, you won't. This principle applies to both good and bad seed! However, there are times when it seems that we don't see the anticipated harvest from the good seeds we have planted. Let's go to a Bible verse that you'll likely never hear in a sowing-and-reaping sermon – Haggai 1:6, "Ye have sown much and bring in little." That one verse is enough to make us stop and re-evaluate all the pat answers we sometimes accept on the topic. Just because we sow doesn't necessarily ensure a bountiful harvest. Israel in the time of the prophet Haggai was proof positive – they sowed a lot but reaped scarcely. The seed-and-harvest principles didn't work for them – and they won't necessarily work for us either if we go about it the same way as did these sixth-century-BC Jews. Furthermore, we don't have to look any further than the parable of the sower itself to see that the seed on the wayside, the seed in the stony soil, and the seed in the weed patch didn't automatically guarantee the sower an abundant harvest. To be totally honest in our understanding of sowing and reaping, we have to candidly face the fact there are situations in which individuals sow good seed but fail to reap a good harvest. Let's consider some of the hindrances that could be responsible for their loss.

Sometimes we fail to reap our harvest because we do not have the proper equipment. A farmer without a combine will not bring in the wheat crop. A boy without a ladder will not get the apple from the top of the tree. As I have traveled through some of the developing nations around the world, I have had the opportunity to witness the way people live in many different cultures, including the primitive conditions in which they harvest their grain. In Nepal, I've watched as the women went into the wheat fields with hand sickles to gather the harvest one handful at a time. With a large sickle, or a scythe, a worker can harvest larger quantities of grain at a time, but he is still limited to one armload at a swath. Dr. Lester Sumrall once wrote of having a vision that prompted him to rethink his efforts as a minister. In the vision, he saw two fields. One was being tended by a little Arab farmer with a camel-drawn plow. He was able to harvest his crop by the basketful. In the second field, an Israeli farmer with a tractor and combine was harvesting his crop by the truckload. The antiquated system would take days to do the same task that the modern equipment could accomplish within a few hours. In the same way, we must determine that we must be properly equipped if we are to bring in the full spiritual harvest in a timely manner.

One of the most important ways of equipping ourselves for the harvest is to be full of the anointing of the Holy Spirit. Jesus was adamant that the disciples not go out into the harvest fields until they were first empowered by the Holy Spirit. (Luke 24:49, Acts 1:8) One of the Holy Spirit's major roles in the life of a believer is to enable him as a witness. He works through several different means in order to fully make each person an adequate witness. One area in which the Holy Spirit empowers our witness is that He makes our lives more attractive to unbelievers through the fruit of the spirit. The Apostle Paul described two radically different lifestyles in the fifth chapter of Galatians. One he called the "works of the flesh"; the other he labeled as the "fruit of the spirit." Even a quick look through these two lists of qualities will allow us to see the attractiveness of the spiritual life and the repulsiveness of the fleshly life. When an unbeliever sees a person living in love, joy, and peace rather than envy, strife, and malice, he is drawn to that person and wonders what is his secret to such a successful and productive life.

When I lived in Indiana, my neighbor had a large apple tree. I walked past it on a regular basis and paid no attention to it. However, in the late summer and early fall of each year I suddenly began to take notice of that special tree. The reason that this poor tree that had never caught my eye all year long was because it was barren; however, now it was the focus of my attention because of the apples it was now producing! Bearing fruit made that tree attractive to me; in the same manner, when our lives begin to bear fruit, we will become attractive to the unbelievers around us.

During my seminary days, I worked as a front desk clerk in Yosemite National Park during the summer break – a position that came with some rather unusual items on the job description. One was to help calm down and re-assign any guests who experienced unexpected "guests" in their rooms – bears! On one particular day, there was an exceptionally heavy load of new guests checking in at the same time we seemed to have an incredible number of bears also trying to check into the rooms. Our lobby soon began to overflow as we became more and more backlogged because of the disruption of the bears prowling around the facility. Before long, our guests were standing outside the front door; eventually the line stretched across the parking lot to the shade of the Douglas firs on the other side of the pavement. When one lady eventually made her way to the front of the line, she smiled at me and asked, "How do you do that?" I was just ready to hold up the room assignment card and show her how I filled in all the blanks and then assigned the room; but I realized that she must be inquiring about something more substantial than how to complete the form, so I asked, "How do I do what?" Her reply was, "Keep smiling in the midst of all this." My response was that it was because I had joy as a manifestation of the fruit of the spirit in my life. I did not have to witness to her – I was a witness because the fruit of the spirit was showing effortlessly through my life.

Secondly, the Holy Spirit empowers our witness in that He gives believers supernatural abilities that draw the unbelievers' attention. The people who would normally totally ignore us will suddenly begin to listen and respond when we lay our hands on them and deliver them from their sicknesses. First Corinthians chapter twelve enumerates nine supernatural enduments that the believer can receive from the Holy Spirit. Many of the gifts are described in action as we read the story of the early church. Acts chapter two tells how that three thousand people were converted when they heard the disciples speaking supernaturally in languages that they had not learned. In Acts chapter three, the response multiples to five thousand when Peter and John ministered healing to a lame man. The story continues to unfold with other miraculous healings, a woman raised from the dead, and a man supernaturally preserved after what should have been a deadly snakebite. In each case, the unbelievers were irresistibly drawn to Jesus through the witness of the power of the Holy Spirit through the believers.

Peter Wagner tells of his days as an instructor of the "Signs and Wonders" class at Fuller Seminary. In that course, he encouraged students to begin to exercise the power of the Holy Spirit in their daily ministry and expect the sick to recover if they laid hands on them and to anticipate that demons really would come out if they used the name of Jesus against them. He testifies that many of his students were graduates who took the class while home on furlough from the mission field. A number of these missionaries wrote back to him after returning to their mission stations to say that they had labored fruitlessly before taking his class, but now they were seeing continual results in their ministries since they were ministering with supernatural signs through the power of the Holy Spirit.

The Holy Spirit also empowers believers in their witness through their words. The very choice of what words are to be said and the boldness to speak them out come from the Holy Spirit Himself. Consequently, the very direction of where to be and what to do when you get there is an important factor in the believer's power to witness through the Holy Spirit.

In addition to the direct intervention of the Holy Spirit, we also need the vision and faith that He inspires so that we can have the insight to envision and then the faith to finance large-scale harvesting projects such as television, mass media, and publications. When there are millions of acres that are producing, we can't be limited to a sickle; we must have the most advanced harvesting skills and equipment available. A Christian without the power of the Holy Spirit will not bring in a harvest of souls. (Luke 24:49)

Others fail to reap because they do not have motivation. "He that gathereth in summer is a wise son: but he that sleepeth in harvest is a son that causeth shame...The sluggard will not plow by reason of the cold; therefore shall he beg in harvest, and have nothing. (Proverbs 10:5, 20:4) In the parable of the talents in Matthew 25:14-30 Jesus portrayed the unprofitable servant and the one who was promoted as having one major the difference – knowing and acting according to the nature of the master. The unprofitable servant knew that the master was one who reaped where he didn't sow; however, he did nothing with the master's money to ensure him a harvest. The promoted servant recognized this prosperity characteristic in his master and acted in faith – expecting that he would have something to reap. Those of us who would desire to be promoted in the kingdom of God need to have only one thing in our hearts – acting in compliance with the nature and will of God. (Ephesians 6:6, Colossians 3:22) We must remember that a double-minded man is unstable in all his ways and will not receive anything – including promotion – from God. (James 1:5-8) Romans 8:6 speaks even more to us about the mental focus we must have – calling it being spiritually minded rather than being carnally minded.

Missionary Seed

I actually became a missionary when I was only a grade schooler. One Sunday, a missionary showed pictures of the destitute people he ministered to in India. When I saw those grainy black-and-white photos projected on the screen, I couldn't help but respond by pledging fifty cents out of my one-dollar allowance. The funny thing is that the next Sunday, the pastor announced that the missions pledges in that service had topped anything in the history of the church. Of course, I was convinced that it was my half dollar a month that made the difference – and it wasn't until years later that I understood better. But the truth of the matter was that my offering certainly wasn't what pushed the congregation over the top, but it certainly did push my destiny much closer to the trajectory God was directing me toward. As a youngster, I didn't have the slightest inkling of the concept that my offering was a seed that would bring forth a harvest – and I definitely had no idea what kind of harvest that it could bring. I doubt that I ever saw any monetary return on that half-a-buck seed, but now I can look back over the more than forty years of ministry in more than sixty nations of the world and marvel at the harvest that has come from that "mustard" seed.

Please allow me to share just one incredible example of where that tiny seed produced unexpected fruit. I had been working in Nepal for several years when my sister and I were doing a tract distribution in a city some distance away from Kathmandu. When my sister handed a man one of our Nepali tracts, he looked at it and recognized that was the same title I had shared with him a couple years prior when we had crossed paths in Kathmandu. After he shared with me that he was a believer, I gave him a full box of the pamphlets to take back with him to distribute in his hometown. Now, holding another copy of that same booklet, he looked up at my sister and proclaimed, "I know Delron Shirley." Not only did he remember the message, he remembered the messenger who shared it with him. After that, my sister began to address me with a line from a song that she felt had been written just for me since I grew up in the Carolinas and was actively ministering in Nepal, "He's known in Carolina and in Kathmandu. It's amazing how one man gets around." But it wasn't just me that was known in Carolina and Kathmandu – it was the seed that I planted in that missionary offering in that little Pentecostal church in a small cotton-mill town in South Carolina that had sprouted and brought forth a harvest many years later and thousands of miles away in Kathmandu and beyond!

Paul made it clear that a transformation occurs in the seed between the time it is planted and the time of its resurrection, "So also is the resurrection of the dead. It is sown in corruption; it is raised in incorruption: It is sown in dishonour; it is raised in glory: it is sown in weakness; it is raised in power: It is sown a natural body; it is raised a spiritual body. There is a natural body, and there is a spiritual body." (I Corinthians 15:42-44) But there is one interesting thing about the parallel between the process of death and resurrection and the principle of sowing and reaping – even though the resurrected body is radically different from the physical body, it is still a body. We see this displayed repeatedly in the resurrection of Jesus. Those who encountered Him had difficulty recognizing that it was Jesus (Luke 24:13-32; John 20:14-17, 20:26-28, 21:4-7); however, they all immediately recognized that the individual they encountered was a man. Likewise, the harvests that we reap from our sowing will come back with a resemblance of the seed that we planted even though the real substance of the harvest is of a significantly different nature. This is a biological principle that Jesus used to illustrate the spiritual kingdom to us.

> So is the kingdom of God, as if a man should cast seed into the ground; And should sleep, and rise night and day, and the seed should spring and grow up, he knoweth not how. For the earth bringeth forth fruit of herself; first the blade, then the ear, after that the full corn in the ear. But

when the fruit is brought forth, immediately he putteth in the sickle, because the harvest is come. (Mark 4:26-29)

This illustration showcases the fact that the rebirth of the seed is radically different from the kernel that is placed in the ground. Blades and ears look nothing like seeds; however, the eventual harvest is filled with corn that is identical to the kernel that was originally planted. The message here is that even though we sow seeds that bring forth harvests of a different nature, there is still the element of the original seed in the new harvest. In that we have already seen that Jesus often likened the harvest to the souls of men, let's explore the connection of sowing monetary offerings that produce a missionary harvest and at the same time produce a financial return.

As a college student, I lived on a very limited budget and helped organize my funds by taking my monthly check and dividing my spending money into four envelopes – one for each week. One night at a special missions rally, I felt impressed to empty my wallet for the offering. This left me a full week behind on my finances, but when I opened my envelope for the next week – much to my surprise – there was twice as much as I had put there! Another experience while I was in college was the night that I felt directed to empty my wallet in a missionary offering one Friday evening. I knew that that meant I would be penniless until the next weekend, but I also knew that my God would somehow take care of me. When I got back to the dorm that night, there was a note on my door directing me to call one of the college professors that night – no matter how late it was that I got in. Even though I hated to call at a rather late hour, I knew that there was an urgency behind the professor's message; so, I returned his call. He greeted me with the offer to work for him the next day. He had received an opportunity to do some side work and needed an assistant – work that I knew how to help him with. Of course, I agreed and met him early the next morning for a full day's work. At the end of the day, he paid me in cash – more than I had put in the offering the night before. That missionary seed brought me an immediate harvest! Not only that – the business opportunity continued for the professor, and he employed me week after week for a number of months, greatly multiplying the seed I had sown. But even more importantly than that was the fact that the money I dropped in the offering plate that Friday night somehow touched a life in some distant corner of the world and produced a changed life that I will never know about in this life but will certainly see the harvest in the next one!

One of my favorite stories on the topic of sowing for missions occurred while I was dean of the Bible college in Indiana. In the backyard of our home stood a giant walnut tree whose upper limbs brushed the very heavens. It was the home of a multitude of grey squirrels that scampered up and down its trunk and ducked into its hollow knotholes only to reappear on the other side of the tree ten feet further down the trunk. This disappearance and reappearance of the furry little creatures became a little discomforting to us since it meant that the tree must be hollow for some major section of its trunk. Since the tree leaned across the roof of our home, we began to feel that it endangered our home and our lives if it were to be blown over. Several severe storms took their toll of limbs from other trees in our yard; yet the giant walnut remained intact even though it rocked and creaked with the violent winds. I talked to several companies about removing the tree but was constantly offered bids that were far beyond my price range. One friend of mine who did tree removal as a sideline volunteered to take it down for us as a favor. But, after climbing the tree and surveying how much actually reached over the house, he descended and rescinded. We tried to postpone the removal until a later date when we might have the extra cash to pay for the service. But when a violent windstorm raged through our area bringing down one of the trees in our yard, my wife insisted that we act immediately before the next storm razed the walnut that, in turn, would crush our home. Since the next week was our annual campmeeting and I knew that I would be busy morning, noon and night, I promised, without fail, to call in a tree company immediately after the conference. In one of the sessions, Dr. Sumrall took a special offering for missions, and I responded by making a five-hundred-dollar donation on my credit card. Now, this was a real step of faith because I knew that I would have to pay around eight hundred dollars to get the tree removed the following week. Now, I was adding an additional obligation of five hundred more dollars. Where would I get an extra thirteen hundred dollars before the end of the month? I had no idea; I only knew that I had to obey the Lord on the missions offering and my wife on the tree removal.

    During the lunch break after the service in which I had made the missions pledge, I walked to my home – which was just across the street from the church — to find a stranger standing in my backyard. I went to find out what he wanted and was greeted with a proposal that I sell him the walnut lumber from the tree. He had been in the area for some other wood procurement and had spotted this tree towering on the skyline. It seemed ideal for his veneer business and he was willing to pay five hundred dollars for it. I quickly settled the deal and arranged for free removal – saving me the eight hundred dollars that it would have cost me to have a tree removal company take it down. I also pocketed the five-hundred-dollar check and used it to pay off my missions pledge. I'm still amazed how that the man was driving in my neighborhood and showed up in my backyard on the very day that I planted a missionary seed by faith. Not only that – but he offered me the exact amount that I had given in the offering!

Remember the story of Dr. Sumrall's visitation from the Lord in Jerusalem that birthed a new phase in his life and ministry? Well, one of the significant elements of that story was that the paper he handed me was almost illegible because his tears had washed away many of his pen strokes and blurred the few words that didn't get totally blotted out. David had forewarned us that the secret to a productive harvest is to water the seeds with our tears as we plant them in the soil, "He that goeth forth and weepeth, bearing precious seed, shall doubtless come again with rejoicing, bringing his sheaves with him." (Psalm 126:6) Even though the sacrificial offerings that I just shared about were painful and required faith and courage, I can't say that any of them brought tears to my eyes. However, there was one day that I literally cried over my offering. When I worked with Dr. Lester Sumrall, I had the privilege to be part of many uniquely world-changing events – one of which was the birth of US-based Christian shortwave radio. Even though there were already organizations using shortwave to broadcast the gospel, none were operating from American soil because the government had restricted the use of this form of communication for government purposes only. But when the Lord spoke to Dr. Sumrall that he was to build shortwave stations in the US to blanket the world with the Good News, not even the US government could resist. And Dr. Sumrall was soon granted the first civilian shortwave license. Before long, there were five facilities broadcasting to every corner of the globe – and one was aimed directly toward Nepal, a nation that I was intimately involved with even though I was able to go there only once a year for about two weeks at a time. When the Lord spoke to me that I could be there fifty-two weeks a year via shortwave, I was ready to jump at the chance – even though the airtime bill would be half my annual salary. I remember feeling like a fool because I could barely get the words out between my sobs when I stood up at the inauguration of the station and made a commitment to the Nepali broadcast. Those tears watered the soil that produced such an abundant harvest that the emerging church in Nepal became known in the following year as the fastest growing segment in the world-wide Body of Christ!

Prophetic Harvest

We have already noted that Amos 9:13 speaks prophetically of a day when the plowman will overtake the reaper and the one who treads out the grapes will overtake the one who sows the seed. This passage seems to be speaking of the end-time harvest of souls that will be so abundant that we will be so busy bringing in the souls that we won't question if the harvest is from our own seed or someone else's. In this prophecy, we are able to get a glimpse of the time when world evangelism will reach a tipping point in that the harvest will come as quickly as the seeds of the gospel are planted. Jesus also predicted this phenomenon in John 4:35 when He directed His disciples' attention to the men of Samaria coming to the well to see Him. When he said that the harvest was four months away, He was speaking of the full growing season. In other words, He was saying that it was really harvest time even though they were still in the planting season! The due season spoken of in Galatians 6:9, "And let us not be weary in well doing: for in due season we shall reap, if we faint not," is not a set time. It is a time of reaping that depends upon the maturity of the crop – a time that might come far ahead of the expected season.

As we have already seen, the harvest of souls should be expected to coincide with a financial return on the monetary seed that was planted to bring in the spiritual harvest. In relationship to this thought, I'd like to convey a prophetic word that was given by the late Dick Mills. But before I share his prediction, let me familiarize you with this man's credentials. I first met Dick when I was working in Yosemite National Park. It was my second summer to serve as an intern in the chaplaincy program in the park, and I had been asked to stay in the park as a full-time chaplain, an incredible opportunity that very few are ever offered – to live and work in one of the world's wonderlands. However, I had one more year of seminary to finish, and I was struggling with the decision to forgo the job offer or try to work out some sort of correspondence program to complete my degree. When one of the Christian park rangers discovered that Dr. Mills was vacationing in the park, he insisted that Dick give the Christian community there one evening of his vacation time to share with us in a home Bible study group. When I came into the meeting that evening, I wound up in the chair right next to Dr. Mills. As I reached out my hand to greet the guest speaker, he startled me with the words, "You are faced with a decision that has to be made within the next week to ten days. Look up Isaiah 30:20, and God will give you an answer." When I turned to the passage, I was amazed that it read, "Thine eyes shall see thy teachers" – a direct answer to my question about returning to campus or doing distance learning. Years later, I wound up sharing the platform with Dr. Mills at a conference. When we bumped into one another in the hotel lobby, Dick immediately followed all the casual small talk that would accompany a greeting with, "From the moment I saw you, I've been hearing the word *transition*." I confirmed his inclination by explaining that I had made the decision to leave the position of dean at World Harvest Bible College and Indiana Christian University that I had held for a quarter century to pursue more missions work – and thought that was the end of the conversation. But God was not finished talking. That evening, Dick was ministering to a couple on the other side of the auditorium where the conference was being held. Suddenly, he stopped in the middle of ministering to the couple and pointed to my wife and me all the way across the room, "God says that He has a house waiting for you." He then went right back to ministering to the other couple. That prophetic word came in February, and by April we were seriously into our house hunt – looking at internet listings and dealing long distance with an agent. We were beginning to realize that anything we would be happy with was far outside our price range. Suddenly, our agent called us to say that she had found something that she was sure we would like and that it was priced far below market value. She encouraged us to come out right away to see the house because she was certain it would not still be on the market in May – when Peggy had planned to fly out to Colorado to do some house shopping. Reminded of the word from God, we decided that it would still be available if it really was the one God had for us. In the time between April and Peggy's visit to Colorado, the sellers turned down two offers. However, they accepted ours even though we offered less than the asking price! Not only has Dick spoken these incredibly accurate prophetic words into my own life, he has also given laser-beam accurate word for all my sons – even though he never met them. Once when we were together, Dr. Mills asked me to write down my sons' names so he could take them to his hotel room and pray over them. That evening, he returned with a page for each of my sons that described them as accurately as if he had lived in our house with them! Well, now that you know that this man's words are not simply random hit-or-miss guesses, let me finally come to the prophetic word he gave concerning the end-time harvest, "God is going to fund the last-day revival so lavishly that televangelists will be embarrassed to try to raise funds." Wow! What an audacious word! But I can't help but believe it. After all, the church has been sowing seed into world evangelism since the day that Jesus gave the Great Commission – and "due season" has to come when there will be an overflowing harvest of souls accompanied with the finances to fund the harvest endeavor!

Teach All Nations Mission

Teach All Nations Mission (TAN) is a global evangelical educational ministry birthed from the teaching ministries of Delron and Peggy Shirley. The name for Teach All Nations Mission was chosen to carefully indicate the exact heart of the Shirleys' mission. TAN's commitment is to establish a solid foundation in national pastors and leaders so they can help enrich their people. This vision is being accomplished by holding national leadership conferences and publishing and distributing Christian teaching materials in English and their local languages.

Someone accurately observed concerning the revival that is occurring in many parts of our world today that it is a mile wide but only an inch deep – the result of energetic evangelism by both missionaries and local Christians. Sadly, there is a marked shortage of teachers who are taking the next step in fulfilling our Lord's directive to teach them how to observe all that He has commanded. Therefore, Teach All Nations Mission has literally taken the words of Christ from Matthew 28:19, "Teach all nations," as its motto and mission statement.

TAN's commitment is to deepen that revival by training the pastors and leaders who then go back and strengthen their congregations. TAN pays for the travel and lodging of handpicked leaders because Delron and Peggy want to invest into their lives but know that these third-world saints could never afford to come at their own expense. TAN always provides the meals for all the guests during these conferences. The ministry also furnishes solid Christian literature in their local language or in English for those who understand the language.

Delron and Peggy realize that the challenge is much bigger than what they can accomplish in person; therefore, they have determined to expand the scope of their vision. One area of expansion includes a scholarship fund that will allow selected individuals to obtain formal education in solid Christian colleges and Bible schools or through correspondence courses. The ministry has also assisted in building a Christian school in Zimbabwe and a Bible college in Nepal. Additionally, Teach All Nations assists the pastors and leaders they work with in times of need such as the tsunami in Sri Lanka, the hurricane in Belize, and the earthquake in Nepal.

Your gifts to and prayers for Teach All Nations will help the Shirleys continue their outreach to Christian leadership around the world.

Teach All Nations Mission
3210 Cathedral Spires
Colorado Springs, CO 8904
719-685-9999
www.teachallnationsmission.com
teachallnations@msn.com

Books by Delron & Peggy Shirley

available at www.teachallnationsmission.com

Bingo – A Fresh Look at Grace
An old joke tells of a man who stood at the Pearly Gates recounting all his good deeds in an effort to gain entry into Paradise. When Saint Peter tallied up the gentleman's score, he did not have anywhere near enough points to qualify. His knee-jerk reaction to the count was, "I'll never get in except by the grace of God." At that instant, the gates swung open and Saint Peter graciously welcomed the gentleman inside. We all know that it is only through grace that we will ever inherit the kingdom of God, but how much do we understand about this all-important subject? Join Bible teacher Delron Shirley as he explores the biblical principle of grace and investigates some of the misconceptions that are current in the Body of Christ today.

Christmas Thoughts
Christmas. The very mention of the word fills our hearts and heads with thoughts – joyous memories, visions of childhood delights, scenes of family gatherings, smells of fresh pastries, tastes of delicious holiday treats, recollections of special friends, strains of favorite carols, and "warm fuzzies" of evergreens, mistletoe, roaring fires, fancy wrappings, shiny decorations, and happy faces. Yes, Christmas is all about thoughts. And we invite you to snuggle up with a hot chocolate and delve into our thoughts about Christmas – and the Christ child whose coming we are celebrating.

Cornerstones of Faith
In our Christian faith, there are also some important cornerstones which serve as foundations to bear the weight of the life we are to build upon them, as indicators or identifiers of who we are as believers, as ceremonial testimonies to the fact that our lives are being built upon Christ, and an unquestionable and invariable standards against which to test and measure everything else in our lives. Proper attention to these essential cornerstones of our faith ensure that our lives rest upon a firm foundation so that we will not fail or falter. Join Dr. Delron Shirley in an examination of the foundation on which our lives must be built.

Daily Devotional Bible Study (five volumes)
This five-volume set of studies takes you on a four-year journey through the Bible. Each manual consists of a walk through the scripture based on studying one chapter each weekday for the fifty-two weeks in a year. Each daily entry includes one verse to memorize. Next comes a short distillation of the basic principle of the chapter and a brief outline of the chapter. This study is intended to be of a rather devotional approach. The Bible study is followed by a simple prayer intended to bring the truth of the chapter into practical application. A section for the reader's notes follows where you can log your own personal revelations and insights about the chapter. A space for logging your own personal spiritual journal (which could include prayer requests, answered prayers, and testimonies) rounds out the daily devotion. The entries for the weekends are a similar format for a study through Psalms. Just twenty minutes a day, seven days a week, fifty-two weeks a year will produce one brand new man in each individual who seriously applies himself to the program and the program to himself.

Daily Ditties from Delron's Desk (Five issues are available)
Each new day comes with its own challenges and blessings. In Daily Ditties from Delron's Desk, you'll enjoy a little pick-me-up to get your day started. So sit back with a warm cup of coffee or tea and see what is in store for you today.

Lessons from the Life of David
In 2004, Michelangelo's famous sculpture, David, went through an extensive cleaning and restoration process in celebration of its five-hundredth birthday. Half a millennium of grime has been removed to once again reveal the majestic splendor with which the masterpiece sparkled when it was first placed in the Piazza Signoria in Florence, Italy. This famous marble statue has often been noted as a most perfect depiction of the human body. And we often think of its subject – the biblical David – as being perfect as well. However, the wonderful thing about the Bible is that it tells the truth -- even about its greatest heroes. They are presented to us as uncovered as Michelangelo's subject, with the only difference being that the Bible depicts its subjects with all their warts, mid-rib bulges, scars, and other defects. In Lessons from the Life of David, Bible teacher Delron Shirley explores both David's triumphs and failures in order to find valuable lessons for our own lives for today.

The Great Commission – DOABLE
While traversing the teeming streets of Kathmandu, Nepal, missionary teacher Delron Shirley was overwhelmed with the throngs of people who had not yet heard the gospel of Jesus Christ. Looking out at the myriad of faces, it seemed like an impossible task to reach them all. Yet, he knew that

Jesus' directive was that the gospel be taken to every human—not just in this one city, but on the entire planet. If reaching this one city seemed like a gargantuan challenge, reaching the planet was beyond imagination! Join Delron in his quest through the scriptures as he explores why the Bible promises that the Great Commission can actually be accomplished and how it is doable in our generation.

Finally, My Brethren
"Finally, my brethren," these are words that seem all too familiar to us when we think of putting on the armor of God for spiritual warfare. However, we often miss the real impact of Paul's message to the church because we have used this as our starting point. But just as we don't start at the top step when we climb a ladder, we can't begin our preparation for spiritual warfare at the last step – putting on the armor. In fact, the Apostle Paul gave us more than fifty steps of preparation to complete before we are ready to get dressed for battle. Join Delron Shirley as he uncovers these often neglected truths. Discover life-transforming truths about your enemy, yourself, God, who you are in Christ, who Christ is in you, and your position in the struggle between the powers of heaven and hell.

The IN Factors
It was offering time in the Sunday school class, and the teacher directed the children to quote a Bible verse about giving as they dropped in their nickels and dimes. A little Afro-American girl with her hair in meticulously cornrow braids grinned from ear to ear as she dropped in the first coin and quoted, "It is more blessed to give than to receive." Her redheaded, freckle-faced friend shyly blushed as she added to the coffer while mumbling, "Give and it shall be given back to you." Next, a young guy tossed in what might have been his "tooth fairy money" as he flashed a broad

smile that exposed the spot where his front tooth had been last Sunday. He then recited, "The Lord loves a cheerful giver." As the fourth little fellow stumbled through, "The seed in the good soil brought forth thirty-, sixty-, and one-hundred-fold return," the teacher anxiously eyed the next child – a first-time visitor who had not been schooled in any of the "giving" passages. Anxious over the fact that the guest would be embarrassed, her heart raced a bit as the offering basket reached him. As the reluctant little tyke begrudgingly plunked in his contribution, he blurted out, "A fool and his money are soon parted."
Although the visitor's quote wasn't from the Bible, it was apparently more appropriate in his own case than any of the verses with which the teacher had coached the rest of the pupils. The truth is that most of us, like the students in the elementary class, have been taught only part of the lesson of what God wants us to know about finances. In <u>The IN Factors</u>, Bible teacher Delron Shirley invites you to join him as he explores some of the lessons that have been taught – but equally important – truths on the topic.

In This Sign Conquer
Marching toward an enemy that he wasn't sure he could defeat, Constantine questioned himself, his army, his military abilities, and even his deities. Then suddenly something happened that changed his life. No, something happened that changed the whole history of Western civilization. He saw a vision in the sky of the Christian cross accompanied by the words, "In this sign conquer." Abandoning his pagan gods and accepting the cross of Christ as his battle insignia, he marched into the Battle of Malvian, defeated Maxentius, and took the throne of the Roman Empire. Since none of us was there in AD 312, we can't be certain how sincere the new emperor was in his acceptance of the cross as his victory symbol. However, we

must know that there are signs and symbols that God has given to each of us to ensure our victory and success in life. Join Bible teacher Delron Shirley as he explores this fascinating topic.

Interface
This book should be viewed as an anthology because each of the seven studies was written at a different time with no deliberate connection to the other six. However, there is a thread running through these independent studies that ties them all together as they communicate different aspects of one unified message – being strategic in our spirituality. The first study deals directly with the interfaces discussed in the Bible where we connect with the world around us, the kingdom of heaven, and the kingdom of darkness. The second study in the series discusses finding the sensitive balance between two necessary interfaces – our need to spend time with God and our mandate to rise up and interact with the world. The third and fourth studies have to do with the biblical truths that we need to understand in order to accurately interface with our God, our world, and ourselves. In the letters to the seven churches of Asia Minor recorded in Revelation chapters two and there, only one of the churches is specifically mentioned as being at an interface; the church at Philadelphia is said to have an open door set before it. Interestingly, this is also the only church that is specifically mentioned as having a relationship with the Word of God. (Revelation 3:8, 10) Therefore, it is significant that we take some time to explore some foundational biblical truths that we must stand upon as we approach the various interfaces set before us. The fifth study takes us through the life of one of our most beloved biblical heroes—David, the shepherd boy who killed a giant and wrote beautiful psalms. Although his life was riddled with one failure after another, he somehow attained the report that he was a man

after God's own heart, which is the key to opening the doors of interface with the world that we learn about in the letter to the Philadelphian church. (Revelation 3:7) Next, we look at what it really means to have heart after the very heart of God – one that Bob Pierce, founder of World Vision, described as being broken with the same things that break the heart of God. Finally, the book concludes with a challenge to never fall short of the opportunities and blessing that God has provided for us as we interface with the One who sent us and those with whom we are to interface.

Israel – Key to Human Destiny

The Jewish people and the nation of Israel are puzzles and enigmas in world politics and human logic. How can it be that a group of people who account for less than one half of a percent of the world's population is responsible for one out of every five Nobel Peace prizes? Israel is so tiny a territory that no world map can even squeeze its name on the space allotted it on the layout, yet this minuscule nation dominates our evening news every night. Why is it that one little country of only a few million people can tie up the wealth, the foreign policy, and the political movements of the greatest nations on the face of the earth? Why is it that of all the ethnic groups in the world, only one bears the stigma (or honor) of having its name specifically coined into a word of hate and antagonism: anti-Semitism? The answers to these puzzling questions lie in the fact that these are no ordinary people and this is no ordinary piece of real estate. These are covenant people living in covenant land. Their destiny is charted by prophetic words from God Himself. Indeed, the saga of all mankind revolves around this people. Israel is the key to the human drama. Join Delron Shirley as he journeys into the past and glimpse into the future in order to understand the present.

The Last Enemy
Fear? Death? Defeated!! The Bible declares that death is our ultimate enemy and that the fear of death is a cruel warden that can hold us in the chains of slavery and bondage throughout our lives. BUT, our enemy Death has met his Waterloo and can no longer hold us in his power. In <u>The Last Enemy</u>, explore Passover weekend AD 33 changed your destiny.

Lessons Along the Way
Welcome to a journey that will lead you across the towering Himalayan Mountains, over rushing waterfalls, and into your own backyard. At each step of the journey and around each bend in the path, you will discover the most exciting thrills of life – not the rush of adrenalin released while crashing through the rapids of the Grand Canyon, not the spine-tingling chill of coming face-to-face with demonic supernatural forces, not the awesome hush of grandeur inspired by the majestic sunsets across the glacier polish of the majestic Sierra Nevada range – although all these and much more are included. You will discover the thrill of hearing the voice of God Himself speaking to you for direction and encouragement. Join us on this fascinating journey through life. Be ready to learn all the lessons along the way!

Living for the End Times
"The end is near!" "Jesus is coming back!" "These are the last days!" We all have heard these prophecies. Sometimes, we've heard them so often and over such a long period of time that they may have lost their impact. Yes, we believe that these are the last days, but we somehow keep living as if we think that things will always keep going as they always have and that nothing is ever going to change. Is it possible that we have given mental ascent to the concept of

the end time but never let it really get hold of our lives? Let's explore what it means to live our lives as if we really believed that these are the end days – after all, they really are!

Maturing into the Full Stature of Jesus Christ
As a child, I learned a little song in children's church: "To be like Jesus, to be like Jesus. That's all I ask – just to be like Him." When I grew up, I realized that there was a whole lot more to becoming like Christ than just singing a little children's song. It has been said that going to church doesn't make you a Christian any more than sitting in the garage will make you an automobile or sitting in a donut shop will make you a policeman. There is a maturing process that we must go through if we ever hope to manifest the true nature of Christ in our lives. That maturing process demands that we have a total transformation in the way we think – that we be brainwashed, if you will. It requires more than just saying the right words; after all a parrot can speak English, but he is not an Englishman. In the same way, we must not settle for just learning the Christian jargon; we must be transformed into the very likeness of Christ through the renewing of our mentalities. You may not be what you think you are, but what you think – YOU ARE! Join Bible teacher Delron Shirley as he investigates how the way we think determines who and what we will be. Learn how your thinking can transform you into the full stature of Jesus Christ.

Maximum Impact
He showed up totally unannounced with no publicity agent, no campaign manager, and no budget to fund a campaign. Yet within three short weeks, he established a viable community of faith that was soon acknowledged and recognized as a role model throughout the world. Who was this man, and how did he flip the world one hundred eighty

degrees on its axis? Join Bible teacher Dr. Delron Shirley as he makes a fascinating quest into the man, his methods, and the mission of a man who left maximum impact everywhere he went.

Of Kings and Prophets – Shapers of the Destinies of Nations

In Of Kings and Prophets, Bible teacher Dr. Delron Shirley invites you into his time machine to travel back through the corridors of time to visit the era of the Old Testament kings and prophets in the nations of Israel and Judah – the men who shaped the destinies of their nations. In walking through the encounters, interactions, and conflicts in the lives of these historical figures, we are constantly reminded of the words of the New Testament writer who said that everything that happened in the lives of these men serves as an example and a caution to us so we can have hope of making a difference in our own generation. (Romans 15:4, I Corinthians 10:11)

Passion for the Harvest – A Missions Handbook

We all know the Lord's statement that the harvest is plenteous but the laborers are few. However, I would like to suggest a little different consideration of the situation: the harvest is plenteous but the laborers are untrained. The cover photograph of a Nepali woman harvesting her grain not only pictures the primitive conditions in which the third world harvests their physical grain, it also helps us get a glimpse of the need for the entire Body of Christ to be trained for the spiritual harvest as well. In Passion for the Harvest, Bible teacher Delron Shirley exposes some of the pertinent truths necessary for preparing us for the challenge of the harvest. Learn how to sow in order to reap an abundant harvest and how to discern the harvest that the Lord is sending your way. Learn how to develop the resourcefulness and the expectant hope necessary to stand steadfastly until the harvest manifests and we discover new truths concerning the tools and the stamina necessary for reaping the full harvest. In short, develop a passion for the harvest!

People Who Make a Difference
Have you ever noticed that there are some people who just seem to stand out from the crowd? Although they may seem ordinary in so many ways, there is just some special something about them that identifies them as unique individuals. Though they may not be the "movers and shakers" that we think of as the ones who can push their way to the top of the corporate ladder, they somehow wind up leaving an indelible mark on their worlds. Let's explore what it is that makes some people the ones who make a difference. Better yet, let's learn how to be those individuals!

Positioned for Blessing and Power
In the first Psalm, David gave us a formula for a life that qualifies for God's blessings – be careful about where you walk, sit, and stand. In the book of Ephesians, the Apostle Paul gave us a formula on how to live in the power and authority of God – be determinate about where we sit, walk, and stand. In <u>Positioned for Blessing and Power</u>, Bible teacher Delron Shirley combines these two principles – one from the Old Testament and one form the New – in a way that can revolutionize your life.

Problem People of the Bible
In <u>Problem People of the Bible</u>, you will meet many of the biblical characters you have had to skip over as you did your daily reading because you simply couldn't understand exactly how their lives figure into the message of God's love and plan of salvation. This insightful story will help you make

sense of their place in the grand scheme of the Bible and the story of God's dealings with the human family.

So, You Wanna Be A Preacher
A distillation of Delron Shirley's twenty-five years of mentoring young ministers and the evaluation of over ten thousand church services and sermons, <u>So</u> <u>You</u> <u>Wanna</u> <u>Be</u> <u>A</u> <u>Preacher</u> covers a wide range of topics from how to recognize and respond to the call into the ministry to tips on preparing and presenting your sermons and on getting them published. Special emphasis is given to helping you understand the minister's job description and recognizing how to manifest the Holy Spirit's presence in your ministry. The minister's personal life including discussion of ethics and etiquette is a major focus in the study. No matter what your ministry or calling, you are guaranteed to get new insights in your role as a minister and gain some helpful hints into effectively serving the Lord and His people.

Tread Marks
Does your life leave a mark on the people you meet and the circumstances you find yourself in? In <u>Tread</u> <u>Marks</u>, you'll learn a number of where-the-rubber-meets-the-road principles of successful Christian living that are guaranteed to ensure that you will leave a positive impression on individuals and society. Based on biblical principles and true life experiences, this book grapples with everyday life issues and presents simple but effective approaches to facing them successfully and victoriously. From the stories of the sinking of the Titanic and an African safari adventures to the expositions on Joshua's conquest of the Promised Land and Joseph's rise from slavery to the second most powerful man in Egypt, you'll be entertained, inspired, and motivated. In <u>Tread</u> <u>Marks</u>, you'll discover how your life can make a lasting impression.

A Verse for the Day (Two Issues are available)
In A Verse for the Day, Bible teacher Delron Shirley brings you a new insight into the Word of God each day with observations about the unique contributions the selected verses can make in our lives. Though the studies of these verses are by no means comprehensive or exhaustive, the fresh insights you'll gain in these daily visits with the Word of God are guaranteed to encourage, challenge, and inspire you in your walk with the Lord.

Women for the Harvest
"God's secret weapon" – that's how many people are coming to realize that we, as women are in the world of ministry. One example is, Dr. Yonggi Cho, who has the second largest church in the world. He has been quoted as saying, "Women are the greatest evangelistic tools. Someday the church will catch on." In this volume, author Peggy Shirley does an in-depth study into the history of why women have been forbidden from taking their God-given place in the church and explores the powerful biblical and historical examples of what happens when women are allowed to use the giftings which God has placed inside them. A revealing study of the scriptures which have long been used to block women from service, coupled with a motivational study on how to break free from the bondages which have held women back and a wealth of practical suggestions and advice -- this book is guaranteed to release you to become a true laborer in God's end-time harvest.

You'll be Darned to Heck if You Don't Believe in Gosh *and Other Musings*

You'll be Darned to Heck if You Don't Believe in Gosh *and Other Musings* is eclectic collection of mediations and musings that address many issues concerning our Christian faith, including exactly what the Bible teaches about hell and who will go there, how prayer works, and how we should understand exactly who Jesus is. This study also takes you on a spiritual journey that delves into such topics as simple advice for Christian leaders and the biblical formula for radical change – both in your own personality and in the complexion of a whole nation.

Lighthearted at times, but always simple and straight forward, this refreshing study makes discovering theological truths from the scripture fun and enlightening. Buckle your seatbelt as you join Bible teacher Delron Shirley as he journeys to such interesting places as Nepal and Nigeria in quest of spiritual insight and revelation. You'll be glad that you came along for the adventure as you discover many simple truths that have always seemed just too difficult to understand.

Your Home Can Survive in the 21st Century

Have you ever heard someone say that we should get rid of old fashion ideas about marriage, family, and morals and add "After all, it is the twenty-first century"? With the rapid decline in traditional values, we might actually begin to question if our home will be able to survive in this new century. But there is good news if we only recognize that what is happening to the family today is a prophetic attack by the forces of the devil and that we are well equipped to fight back and conquer! You home can not only survive – it can thrive!!